SOLITUDE

REFLECTIONS OF A MONK

WLADIMIR DIAS
17/10/2014

By Wladimir Moreira Dias

Universo Inteligente

Ansiedade zero

Templo da Malícia

Vencendo o Mundo

Coração Partido

Sonhos & conquistas

Pulsação - Uma Viagem Rumo ao Desconhecido

O manuscrito secreto do rei Salomão

O Khan - A elite dos guerreiros

Alquimia das Emoções

Ritual da maturidade

Pulsação e o manuscrito secreto do rei Salomão

Pulsação - Uma questão de sintonia

Intelligent Universe — What is the ultimate fate of our universe

A era da solidão

Pulse — Un viaje hacia lo desconocido

Páginas em branco

Napoleon — The fish

SOLITUDE

REFLECTIONS OF A MONK

"Who can find pleasure in solitude?."

"This book is dedicated to a special someone."

Thank you the collaboration and confidence of everyone who helped me make this project a reality.

AUTHOR'S NOTE

The nature has given us a very special gift and that helps us in our journey through life, which is our capable to forget.

This fantastic ability helps us to forget much of everything that has gone wrong in our lives ... Our tears ... Our pain. What were ... What we wanted to be ... This is because life is art of renewal and takes care to give us other mementos, other things to think about and worry...

Today we are facing the evil of the century within each of us.

All somehow are embraced by some of the tentacles of solitude.

Some talk a lot, but remain silent about intimate aspects of their lives.

The loneliness in small doses stimulate reflection, but the radical loneliness stimulates the depression. When we talk about loneliness, we don't have to avail ourselves of the only monologue. We can learn to talk and get the exercise through art.

There will always be a silent conversation between the actor on stage and the guy in the dark of the audience, between the visitor of a Museum and the painter in his Studio, the writer and his unknown reader.

Ah! The books ... without any doubt, they are the most thought provoking and anarchistic in my opinion. Read, and your silence will gain voice. Good read!

"The education for life should include also lessons of loneliness."

VISITING THE MONASTERY

I was a bit introspective when I heard, in the distance, a repetitive noise of Horn.

So I already could imagine who would be, in fact, couldn't be somebody else, because this was the hallmark of the arrival of Joseph, a young Manager and brother-in-law of Iohan.

He, a few years ago, decided to become adept at a doctrine from origins monastic coming from some monks who inhabited this island at the end of the 9th century and he sought, the few times that always happen during the Saturdays and were held in a former monastery located near to the village, in the vicinity of the farm.

At this location I could see gathered dozens of people to participate in activities related to meditation

During his advances, always told me that these practices only had advantages, it undoubtedly among the most efficient techniques when we seek our inner balance, and if it practiced regularly can be seen as a really powerful weapon against our emotional instability.

In my view, despite he always is being a bit flustered, I considered him   almost an expert on issues related to meditation, because he really showed me how much like and know about these immersive methods.

 Within of this his persuasive posture he used to tell me:- in these my moments searching to improve, thanks to God, I began to think less of all my emotional oscillations, which both tormented me. -What do I did for that? - Asked himself and placing his right hand on his heart. – I think it was just a matter of positioning even, a way to perceive some things, today i can understand better about them, facing as a mere transitory mental state in my life.

After that, Joseph stayed crestfallen for a few seconds and then emphasized: – Actually I think tricky for all of us this quest for inner peace and, frankly, sometimes we really need professional help to guide us in this conquest – completed. Joseph showed an impulsive personality and, along this line, suddenly decided to ask me if I had any idea about the three most difficult things of life. I, a little surprised by your question, I commented that I didn't have a clue.

Then he told me with a smile

- Get the peace of mind, take advantage of the time and really find your better half. -Hum! I think I agree with you – I replied.

After a short break, Joseph continued with their reflections.

- You know, from the beginning, what motivated me to attend the sessions in the monastery was the fact of that they show me some innovations, which I thought was interesting in relation to traditional meditation, which, without any doubt, is a direct result of the strong influences that had the order Charterhouse, one of the most traditional and known in the West.:

Today she is already quite widespread on the island, being widely used by those who meditate there, in order to seek inner peace.

As a result, he decided to highlight based on his own experience, the strong influence of anxiety on our emotional balance.

This was the persuasive Joseph, always with their many arguments.

Iohan, which was near, agreed with the statements of his brother-in-law, telling us that really, in all his studies related to the human psyche, considering also some seminars which he had participated, the anxiety was always presented as the basis of all our emotional ills, and has continued to ...

-She is not restricted to any particular life phase or to any group of people, because their characteristics if instill in all human situations, working directly at the heart of our emotions, causing a kind of mental unrest that seems to have no objectivity.

At this point, I realized that Iohan was a bit excited about the content of our subject and continued to explain his experiences, I and Joseph only listened intently.

I particularly like a lot of these issues that focus on human emotions and Joseph also demonstrated satisfaction in how information flowed very good from Iohan.

Suddenly, at that moment, a heavy rain began to fall on the farm, interrupting our discussion and Iohan had to take care of the various running chores that was happening nearby.

I and Joseph followed ahead to the balcony of the mansion and he continued talking to me, because he still wanted me to explain more about meditation techniques developed in the island.

But due a strong storm that began to reach the place where we were on the porch, we decided to continue our conversation in the room.

As soon as I entered I realized that on the coffee table in the corner of the room there was a small bottle with a few drops of liquor prepared by Iohan and I took it, without delay, to serve me this remnant of liqueur, mint flavored.

After taking a SIP, wanted to make it clear to Joseph who, though find meditation a magnificent technique, had me convinced that could never reach their highest level, known as the State of "enlightenment", but, anyway, I also think that even when it is practiced in a more superficial level can we promote or contribute in our quest for emotional stability.

– You know, Joseph, I think our contemporary life style demonstrates a lot of complexity, when we seek the feeling of happiness, because as it is formed by several plans, we almost always running also in their various obstacles, which hinder our good socialization, regardless of context. So, I am always looking for keep me with an open mind, seeking to learn new techniques to help me achieve the best possible balance, making my life more productive and happy.

Focusing a little more on human relationships, for example, at work, in accordance with the experience we have accrued over the years, I think must be necessary for an individual to build a successful career, not just his know-how or the equipment available, but is of paramount importance (weighs a lot) for this success the quality of people that we meet, i.e. this future success, of course, is not simply the product of such skill he had but mostly how you managed to harmonize with those people who at one time or another of his professional life took part, contributing or slowing your way.

If the individual can develop this skill in dealing with people, in society, the possibility of having emotional fluctuations decreases too.

On the other hand, when you don't have this ability, your problems will multiply, eventually leading to alienation and social antagonism; the pressure will be greatly increased, undermining that minimum balance, so necessary for your constructive and development of spiritual realization.

In my opinion, this is because the primary goal of our life is essentially linked to the concept of human relationships, and the more you realize this essence becomes clearer his vision of cosmic prosperity, resulting in a social life more meaningful and fruitful.

After my reflections, suddenly decided I would visit this monastery as spoken by Joseph, because I ended up feeling me a bit indebted to him, given his persistency so that I knew this place.

Thus, on Saturday I went with him, in order to participate of these meditation sessions. Arriving there, he introduced me to an old monk practically blind. I was very curious and decided to ask him why in the early 9th century monastic the island had been chosen.

And he promptly replied, emphasizing that at that time these monks had sought to live the Gospel the way as perfect as possible.

By reason of choose this lifestyle, were baptized by some as "the seekers of the path to Christian perfection".

One of these monks, called Gracian, was really passionate about Christ, was always taken from enthusiasm for the pursuit of Christian perfection, and to achieve this ideal, renounced the world and to their lusts and immersed himself to explore other lands, until he found this fantastic Island, isolated in the Atlantic, where he settled, bringing his fellow hermits, who shared the same ideals that he.

Certainly, only the time witnessed and the best protagonist of this beautiful lifestyle started by those monks, guided by Gracian, at the end of the 9th century.

Without doubt, in the film of the time, shall have been captured every detail of daily life of the monks, as if they were part of a dimensional film, showing an example of everyday life; and certainly recorded the expression of their faces too, the rumor of the steps in the great halls of the monastery, which was built by them, with a arduous and painstaking work defined through of a proven union of this team.

On this site, today, people find the proper orientation to cultivate a stronger spirit, cheerful and courageous. Here we believe that mankind needs a lot of meditation, under penalty to succumb by the technique without ethics and progress without God. - Young man, always keep in mind that freedom is the space that happiness needs. Agreed, with a brief nod.

Then I said him that I had really appreciated all the information and after, despite having enjoyed the entire environment, I preferred didn't participate in any of the sessions that happened in the various rooms of the monastery, just walked the halls, just aiming to know the various steps in this process of meditation always followed by so many people, being that each of them lasted for several hours, always under the guidance of the monks.

When I saw them punctuating some changes about the their techniques, I understood the dynamics and direction of his contemplative lives.

I think they've been seduced by a greater mystery, that still don't quite understand.

In one of the halls of the monastery, I saw a small frame with the following sentence: "this is the quiet:" let the Lord speak to us a word equal to it ". Advantaged the moment, I wrote down in my Smartphone.

Today, here writing, I'm sure I will never forget the penetrating susceptibility that I witnessed in that monastery, which appeared in the force of night on their "solitude sound", the sound of the rain, wood burning and crackled in the greenhouse, in the details of the fruit on the tray, the glass of water on the table, in the basin that swayed and the man who removed snow in one of your entries.

Down the Hall, in one of the most isolated, halls could hear some monks who sang very softly, a type of song very similar to the Gregorian.

I learned that the three mottoes that moved the life of these monks more extremists were the silence, the solitude and simplicity, except for their moments of chanting. To my right there was an entry for a small chapel inside the monastery and I decided to pray there and raise a little my soul.

At that night, in the end of the session, certainly will not go to forget the rhythm of those bells and how beautiful were those ringtones.

But what impressed me most at that location is that nothing would happen hastily and that rhythm, along with the silence, seemed to spend a lesson, because in that moment I realized clearly the whole intention of this frame, not just the rumors of silence, but mainly by the technique they used, seeking to educate the look of those people who stood by.

The purpose of these monks was to improve the perception of these people for small signals, the details of life, which almost always escape of those who live under the rule of rush and the quest for success.

Indeed, during these hours I remained at the monastery could realize the numerous and rich details of the work of these monks, in the kitchen, in the round-house, the rhythm of his quiet power, gathering for prayer, the scene in which the monk fed the cat, the joy and gratuitousness in the act to go downhill on the snow.

Without forgetting, of course, the images of nature in that region so splendid, as the trees that danced under the rhythm of the wind and also a beautiful sky that embraced all over that place, seeming to search to protect the landscape.

Late at night we returned to the farm and, in the car, I thought as I would have loved to do this tour, because he had surpassed all my expectations. Told Joseph that create the serenity in life is very important, especially for a big-city dweller like me, because the modern urbanization, foreign expansion and the growing mechanization increases the complexity and decrease the parsimony of our lives, and completed:

– Only when we are calm is that we are able to see things as they really are.

I really think just when we are quiet we can mirror the truth of things, demonstrating a pure creativity, that only expresses himself through a serene and harmonious mind.

In my view, although the State of serenity is part of our life, she necessarily needs to be continuously structured in our minds, because if neglected can become almost wild, making us lose our good essence and favoring the chaos in our lives.

Joseph then told me that he had just read an excellent book, written by an Indian Mud, which offered many words of wisdom, and that certainly could help me a lot in my reflections.

In this book, exemplifies very well this issue of serenity and question:

– What is the serenity? Will be the dawn of a glorious day, with sunshine through the leaves, whose silence is sometimes broken by the sound of the birds, who wake up amidst the scent of dew wet grass?

- Is it really the much longed-for serenity? He retorted.
I thought a bit and told him:
-Sincerely, Joseph, sometimes I'm skeptical about whether the serenity really exists in our soul, for this achievement is very difficult.

- Joseph then told me:

- This book talks about it too, and explains that, like nature gives no jumps, changes of our most ingrained habits also happen very slowly. Become pacified is an exercise in continuous re-education.

One must begin to cultivate patience and silence of the mind in our daily life, until this process will be installing and getting stronger.

Every man is pacified if not disturb himself by details day-to-day, softening their impact on your ego, and over time the real peace settles within him, acting like a bubble that protects him from the chaos of modern life.

– Actually, Joseph, I think you always need to protect ourselves of this incessant toil of modern life, in our quest for superfluous and pleasure exorbitant causing imbalances in our emotions and torments us both.

Joseph, I think all of us, in some way, we are seeking to conquer a well-ordered spirit, but the shape of this achievement will depend on the ability and preparedness of each in this life.

PROLOGUE

Loneliness is the art of encounter with the existential void.
That void has a double meaning.

One is the existence of a metaphysical meaning; the other is the absence, of the loss of something important.

The freedom is a solitary discovery, what explain why many try to avoid it.

The loneliness is a feeling that generates anxiety and that puts us in front of a gate in an inner world where the key is the sense in the world, the why of things, the questions we do and for which we can't find answers, but can also be an experience of transcendence.

Everything in life is a process of learning level, that is, from the inside to the outside. We must have the courage to learn from her and not just reject it. Reject our solitude is the same as rejecting our shortcomings, our human miseries.

There are people who will do anything to avoid talking about loneliness, about illness, about human miseries.

At the bottom, is just an attempt to avoid the contact with reality.

Individually speaking, our true distinction is established by how we deal with loneliness, defining our feeling of freedom or of abandonment that her stems, depending on the way in which we interpret, whereas consciously or unconsciously, our perception of the origin of our existence.

The man becomes real when it accepts the loneliness as the price of their own freedom. And becomes inauthentic when interprets the loneliness the abandonment, as a kind of disregard of God or of life about him.

With this open hand of his own existence, becoming a stranger to himself, putting himself at the service of others and diluting the impersonal and remaining in life, just as a supporting character of their own history. " Being authentic is the one who is responsible for your life, the leading actor, the architect owner the masterpiece of his life.

When you have good emotional relationships, loneliness is great and works in our favor.

Nobody demands anything from anyone and so both grow.

All people should be left alone from time to time, to establish an internal dialogue and find your personal strength.

In solitude, the individual understands that the harmony and peace of mind can only be found within himself. Take a brief moment to close your eyes, open your heart and feel all that comes from inside him, in his natural and healthy silence. Take care of you.

#CONSIDERATIONS

I'm always traveling for work, either by Brazil and also outside, routine that I want, which I define time, time to devote phases chosen as the dance and the moment is related to love, affection, work, money, video games, guitar, drawing, coffee, poetry, texts, books, friends, family visits, visits in my house, I try get used to it.

When the latter happens it's always kind of weird, and I feel that already both got used in caring for me, almost always far and sometimes when i have someone around...

Just don't get used to it and I believe that we should not do and get used to the loneliness by herself, since it only really are not.

We are with us, and seek always to be a good company to deal with us, enjoy us, live with happiness in the heart and not just survive, when we lack that feeling of feeling yourself, ambiguous redundancy weird in figure of speech, but this is real life for those who live alone traveling the world, but not alone and, when not, with that roll, romance, dating, affair, which both want, if i desire love, that maybe, for now, I haven't got somebody to pick up that copy of the key that is in a cup of that famous hypermarket, there still on top of the desk. A matter of time, today, this is our, ourselves and with us.

WORDS OF SOLOMON

There is a proper time for everything. There is a season for everything under heaven ... A time to be born and a time to die ... A time to plant and a time to reap what you sowed... A time for struggle, a time to heal the wounds. A time to break down and another to rebuild ... A time to weep and a time to laugh. A time to grieve and another to dance for joy. A time to scatter stones and a time to gather them. A time to embrace, and a time to walk away if ... A time to search and another to lose ... A time to store and to distribute to ... A time to rend and sew. A time to be silent and another time to talk ... A time to love and a time to hate ... A time for war and a time for peace.

God inspired the wisest King and rich to compose brilliant sayings full of advice for you to prosper in all areas of your life.

Nothing is off limits in this fabulous book of the Bible. The comment is practical, current, and spiritual impact. There is nothing better around.

SOLITUDE

REFLECTIONS OF A MONK

The sandals of the master resounded deafly on the stone steps that led to the basements of a former monastery, built in the tenth century had a face veiled by a hood and going down slowly aided by his cane toward the his quarters.

At the end of the stairs, was a long underground corridor, which had dozens of doors and after a few steps, stopped in front of a heavy wooden door ajar, addressing without delay, to a small desk, where he sat and began to make some notes on a great book, almost as old as him.

Life is a whirlwind of emotions and our existence is a splendid miracle.

This our brief stay here, we can never escape our trials, because the pain will always burilando our hearts, while we live.

Who does not know that famous phrase of Christ "Do your part and I'll do mine."

This distinction is not easy, but it's always an opportunity to learn and also rethink our attitudes, because only complain of life, is to evade the responsibility it imposes on us.

We are intelligent beings on this planet and we should get rid of everything that impedes our progress. After accepting life is not complaining, but, being in her presence and understanding that its ongoing transformation, it is the only possible way to the light of knowledge...

This action and reaction happen at all there, from the atom to the universe at all times, representing a natural movement of life.

If for any reason, we try to ignore these your changes, by changing things, even before they are really ready for this, surely this battle is already lost, already unprepared to face this system we live in, will mean certain defeat.

The old monk was alone in her room and continued writing with his trembling hands ...

We need to understand that life takes its course and for her, we are just another element of nature, and therefore we have to take care of ourselves, using our main weapon., Ie, our cognitive capacity and by it, we need to make a difference for things to happen in order to favor our lives.

We should always get rid of the dust of prejudice and see things more clearly, to then evolve.

There are two primary energies that are the basis of this our temporal life: change and maintenance. Both are equally important, and transmits the change in an outcome of transformation and evolution, since the maintenance, conveys the rhythm and eternity.

When seeking the acceptance of things as they are, does not mean we have to blindly accept some kind of destiny, nor should we become victims of circumstance, as this would be accommodation. And accepting means not accommodate it, however, when we recognize the value of true inner acceptance, this approach frees us and empowers us, to change or not a given situation, according to what is best for us.

Everything changes the whole time and this is the one great fundamental truth of life. If we were ready to accept this fact, surely we would suffer much less in front of events, as it continually changes, we realize that these things are what they are or how they are acting, too shall pass.

For those who have learned the art of acceptance, know that this card game called life, there is no place for accommodation because you need to play the hand that received the best possible way and nothing can prevent the light of knowledge to reach us.

Throughout our history, the extraordinary men who appeared, depended much of the time in which they lived to stand out, because all things have their time and this case was no different. Not worth fighting simply because this is not enough.

When we seek to accept things as they are in life, it is much easier to analyze what is their real purpose at that time and why they are the way they are. This attitude helps us to better choose our direction, because we have more clarity and therefore also a better understanding of the situation created.

Within this context, then we are better able to define if let things happen naturally or if they will fight.

As with all rules, there is always an exception, the art of living also has its.

There is always a factor that should be considered and what some call luck, or being in the exact place at the right time with the right person, it makes much difference in any possible success in life. However, this good luck also has its rule, because not everything is by chance, to the wise, the effort can help a lot.

When we are favored by these moments that happen a few times in the course of our lives; the differential of some minds, that radiate light like the eyes of reason Lynx and masterfully mostly darkness, can make all the difference. this victory.

Therefore will be using important skills and that certainly will be your aid in this quest for personal fulfillment as desired.

Now, those other people who react according to the occasion, representing the overwhelming majority of people end up hurting themselves and often compromising definitely your future and your happiness.

The life story teaches us that not everyone had the time they deserved and that many had failed to enjoy it.

Some others were even worthy of better days, but as success does not always triumphs, were succumbed amid the antics of a society that judges us more by our defects than by our virtues.   Human life is a constant struggle against the malice of man's wit and often struggle with the stratagems malice and dissimulation. For this becomes important if develop keen intelligence to always to protect with caution in any possible double play.

Life is a school and for those who know how to enjoy their teachings, soon learns to better evaluate the real intention of the people who surround them.

There is much to know, but life is too short and if you do not know, do not live well. It is therefore a special ability to learn very many and those who cannot have wisdom as servant should have it at least as a companion because the effort and the capability should walk together.

The dynamic of this our life, we need to quickly identify our top quality and doubling its use as a rule the discernment and courage to others.

The old monk, with his wrinkled face still obscured by broad hood, still writing, despite the late hour.

About this our judgment, we need to better understand our origins, to be more balanced.

Although religious, not contempt Science and I know that she believes that the basic bricks that make up our universe are based on a single particle, known as the "God particle" and penetrate within the deepest core of the proton, an the components of the atom and can be considered as the basis of all that exists.

She believes that through its manifestation of this was possible to create matter and motion, the substance and the

She believes that through its manifestation of this was possible to create matter and motion, the substance and the strength, also enabling the interaction of a third element, represented by the intelligence.

However, for this existence was first necessary to define all the conditions for the development of life, and the first thing thought to top it all, was undoubtedly the creation of light.

Therefore, we can understand that God by his very nature, is very light and all its action merely consist in an act, the manifestation of the light of truth. For a little we understood God better, we must first truly be free, because only this way we can develop our creative spirit and find that sacred place within us where the divine spark of eternal life and our hopes that pulses but this is not an easy task and few succeed.

Now when we enter the courage within, which is a more humane situation, we must also learn to be practical, then develop our abilities to adapt to the environment where we live, but always bearing in mind, never losing his composure and or respect for himself.

The first rays of sun now began to bathe his chambers, expressing a clarity that the old master is unaccustomed as he wrote in his big old book.

Then after closed, and was moving away, letting out a faint smile.

The other day scouring the monk in the parlor some books, bumped an ancient scroll and somewhat curious to read methodically, reflecting for hours, realizing that it was the secret scroll of King Solomon, imagine that all the time already lost.

Despite its incredible discovery, did not outline any fanfare, just sat quietly on a wooden bench in his favorite corner and after some more time for detailed analysis, seeking the veracity of the document, decided in a surprising way, by just registering what had just reading in his old book, happily returning to their routine as much of a simple solitary written, strangely without question as such preciousness had come to his hands.

I had imagined that moment to have been some kind of miracle from heaven, and after looking at the sun's rays emanating from the small window, went to his desk and continued to write ... Not everything must be speculation: it takes action. The wisest are the easiest to fool: though they know extraordinary things, ignorant, know nothing of the ordinary necessities of life.

The contemplation of sublime things leaves no room for the ordinary, and, as they ignore the basic things of life - where all the others are so insightful - or are admired, or are considered by the ignorant vulgar superficial.

Therefore, the sages have a bit of traders, not enough to be duped and ridiculed. All that your hand finds to do, do it with all your heart. Learn be practical: it cannot be the highest concern of life, but it is most needed.

What good is knowledge if it is not practical? Who is wise seeks to learn, but fools are satisfied with your own ignorance. When wisdom enters into your heart, and knowledge is pleasant to your soul, Discretion shall preserve thee, and keep thee intelligence. Nowadays, true knowledge is in knowing how to live.

Do not confuse the taste of others. Causing grief rather than pleasure. Some try to please and end up harassing, because they do not understand the character of others.

The same thing that flatters offends some others. What was considered a favor turns into grievance. Sometimes, it would have cost less pleasing than bored.

Lose the gratitude when it is unknown how to please others.

If you do not understand someone's character, you can not satisfy him.

That's why some thought be praising when in fact insulted: a well-deserved punishment. Others plan to please with eloquence, when in reality bore the soul of others with his loquacity.

Not trust his own reputation without pawning other people's honor.

The damage for talking too much and the advantages of silence should be reciprocal.

When honor is involved, the deal should be together, and must ensure the reputation of another.

It is best not to rely on others, but if you do, it is with art, so he yields space for prudence and caution. Divide the risk to both follow the same interest and confidant does not become a witness against you.

If you let the ax missed the cut and not the edge, will have to work much harder.

It is smarter to plan before acting. Know how to ask. There is nothing more difficult for some and easier for others.

There are those who cannot deny; it does not take a lock pick to deal with them.

Others have not always to first response, in which case it required skill.

With all of them, act timely. Surprise them when they are happy, after delighting the mind and the body.

The wise man hides his wisdom, the fool announces its ignorance.

Nothing belongs to us beyond time, the only abode of those who are homeless.

Life is precious, and it is so unfortunate waste it on lofty tasks.

Do not overload nor occupations, nor envy. Without wood a fire goes out; without gossip a quarrel is over. You run over to smother the life and spirit.

Some extend this rule to learn, but who does not know does not live.

Do not begin to live where it should end. There are four mysterious things that I cannot understand:

The eagle flying in the sky, the snake crawling on the rocks, the ship that finds its way into the sea and the love between a man and a woman.

Some rest at the beginning, leaving fatigue towards the end.

Make yourself the essentials first, then if there is time, the accessory.

Some want the victory before the fight.

For a monk, loneliness is an option, it is not boring, it is a remedy.

It is in solitude that caught the best conversations of our lives, because only in absolute silence you can hear the voice of our own heart.

It is when the mouth is shut, there is no one to exchange words nor smiles, we must look to ourselves.

Note that people who hate being alone, are the most desperate for escape, as well as children who flee lessons given by parents.

Loneliness is a luxury, not a waste.

It us closer to ourselves, as nothing else does.

The best ideas will certainly emerged in these introspective moments and locked in an empty room.

Books arise, of course, by observing the world but thereafter required number of times of reflection and is loneliness.

Because we are what we are, without fear or shame.

Who's afraid of being alone, fear of repression itself.

Afraid of the trial itself.

But who can grow without an internal fight?

Must fight our own battles to develop our strategies of war.

Crying, read a book, invent theories about the universe, create a poem, studying all matters of history and try to connect facts, sing a nostalgic song, open any page of any book and from that stretch, try to remember the sequel.

The loneliness is a gift, not a debt! Talking to yourself, laugh at the mirror, staring at the ceiling, making a work of art, see photographs.

Does anyone doubt that these are the moments in which we find ourselves?

Does anyone doubt that the cry, reflect on happiness; in the book, about meta language; in music, what were some time before and the mirror of who we are today?

It is a meeting of the self with the self.

And you want someone to understand us better than we know ourselves? Loneliness has more advantages than you think.

There are things that bind us to the skin and never drop out us.

They are images, sounds, smells.

Sometimes small gestures, questions that make us, we hear conversations.

Today at breakfast I remembered it.

I do not know why or what prompted me to do so.

But suddenly, wham. And there she was beside me looking at me in my reverie.

We never talked, never knew his name and sometimes even doubt until it has existed. When this doubt assails me open my wallet and try your outline deep inside that compartment where I keep some papers in an old trunk and occasionally make me lack. And it is there, round, smiling at me. I'm glad to have her there, has me a strange feeling, as in some other situations where I have felt more crestfallen, sad or laden with problems and uncertainties, the simple contact, the act of feel it, grab it and touch it has given me almost immediate relief from these ailments.

Already keep a few years ago, I'm not sure how many, nor is it important.

It was a Sunday. Had gone to church, which was completely full.

She pretty, all dolled up, a soft background music anticipating the arrival of my fellow monks.

It was Sunday but it was not any Sunday.

It was Easter Sunday.

Everything around was celebration and joy.

The procession leaving shortly.

Early risers rockets had agreed that the armed populace of great faith soon be concentrated in the churchyard, preparing throats, soulless to sing and cry: Alleluia, Alleluia.

I was early as usual taste.

With time to see, hear and appreciate the joy that this day deposited in people.

Before the Mass started the church was already full. overfill.

When the ceremony began hardly could make room for someone else.

It was then I saw her.

It was the side of my foot, with great suffering and supported by a cane.

Bent by the weight of age.

She wore a black skirt, a white blouse and black cardigan over also.

The chest a wire with a medal with two entwined hearts. Beneath Hearts phrase:

I was born for you.

It was then that our eyes crossed. Smiled.

That smile crossed me whole was sown in me like that.

I had never felt such a chill through my body, a feeling of purity that seemed to make me levitate.

I looked away but his smile still live in me.

I got up and gave her my seat.

I stood.

He thanked me kindly and I kept wrapped in the magic of that smile.

The Mass continued.

Beside me she was praying fully concentrated.

Kneeling. Communed.

At one point I saw her play the hand to the chest and the medal he had there.

The Mass ended and hear the confusion of departure.

Suddenly I felt a hand grab mine and something round and metal to be deposited therein.

Involuntarily closed my hand and looked around. Did not need to look to know what it was.

In the confusion of the exit tried to reach it.

Thank you, tell him that he could not accept.

I could not.

I saw it already at the exit door.

Perky looked through the crowd.

Seemed to pass by people without touching them.

He turned back and smiled again.

Never saw her again.

Sometimes I doubt that really existed.

Sometimes eye and she is beside me smiling at me.

Other times is stored in the wallet.

Today when I drank coffee I felt his presence beside me.

In my daydreams, she gently touched my hand and told me:

-Give me...

I looked and was no longer there.

A huge sun took care of me and a miraculous peace enveloped me.

Enveloped us both.

Are you my hand and smiled.

The same beautiful smile and suit for five, ten, fifteen, twenty years.

Caught you in hand and leave there the medal:

I was born for you.

As a monk by vocation, I learned that I can walk alone, but by no means am a lonely person.

I also have my moments of emotional fluctuations and memories despite their advanced age I am still a young man, of course not biologically, but psychologically.

And often, depression causes me suffering a series of periodic, very characteristic mainly within a moody personality.

I go through weird emotional fluctuations or changes in mood.

Sometimes I feel on top of the world.

I'm euphoric and exuberant ready to accomplish anything.

I feel light and joyous, but often this mood of expansion is followed by the opposite mood, contraction and depression.

In these years the monastery developed my self-help techniques that help overcome these moments, stimulating and redirecting my thoughts.

When I find myself in this state of depressed mood, usually suffer a lot by creating feelings of guilt and inferiority.

For me life has lost its charm, his confidence proves extremely compromised, until finally begins to feed nihilistic desires.

Life seems a dark night that will never end, assuming often extreme proportions that without proper guidance it can reach even one degree often pathological.

However, with proper counseling, it will lead undoubtedly to prevent distortion of these states ideas that create those terrible emotional instabilities, and that all of us at one time or another in our lives witnessed or felt to a greater or lesser degree, showing us that to some extent this is completely normal.

It is at this point that our intellect becomes crucial to achieve that heralded minimum inner balance and that allows us to enjoy a social life.

This balance will occur mostly in that understanding we consciously or unconsciously, the true causes of these emotional fluctuations, to which we are continually exposed, leaving us better prepared so we can beat them, for this is an endless struggle and lasts a lifetime.

Our minds, witness in one day, many situations that affect us positively or negatively on our mood, even when we do not realize, these social interference are always active.

In general, our mood is extremely susceptible to all sorts of outside influence and often for one reason or another, do not manage these huge amounts of emotional charge we received, until all these flows and external emotional ebbs ultimately define the our mood, creating an unconscious psychic atmosphere, in which we are no longer masters of our own humor, which becomes a simple product of the external environment in which we are exposed, almost always resulting in a bad mood.

In contrast, there are also easy periods in our lives when all the winds are blowing in our favor, the outlook is bright, the joy of living is spontaneous and the will to perform is unbreakable. This could be one famous "our moment" that happens a few times in our lives, and therefore, it is prudent to take full advantage of it, but always taking due care not to become overconfident and end creating an opinion of himself, far short of its reality, which certainly will bring strong future frustrations.

Many times when a person gets involved by the enthusiastic excitement that apparent success, which often leads him to commit excesses, mistreating others and antagonizing many interests, causing what is called social reflux, ie, a strong reaction from people who the fence, creating a never ending atmosphere of dismay on his back, eventually obscuring further their mental horizon, contributing to an imminent worsening of possible depressions.

However, to the best prepared individuals, any antagonism is always seen as another challenge to be overcome.

The life force flows in them as a strong and elastic spring that cannot be suppressed forever and it matures and becomes increasingly stronger. In a generic way, our emotional mood largely determines our way of thinking.

In a moment of deep sorrow can only perceive sad facts and so does most joyful times, only when we realize facts that lead to a euphoric mood.

It is always desirable to act with prudence during these phases of rise of emotional mood.

The big secret to keep away from depression, based on how we view the various panoramas that are formed in the course of our lives and how we manage them, ie, the preparation of each one makes a difference in the final result of this endless fight against depression, meaning more or less balance emotional balance.

It is always important to keep in mind, especially in those moments of complete despair in which they cannot intellectualize absolutely nothing, that everything passes and nothing is really as fundamental, that can supplant importance in the lifetime opportunity.

Meditation is undoubtedly one of the most efficient techniques when seeking inner balance and regular practice can become a powerful weapon against depression. Insofar as the individual improves this technique, he begins to consider depression as a mere transitory mental state, making it very easy their friendship with her.

Efficiently used by those who meditate, as you tend to fall into a deep depression, is to seek in meditation, the strength they need to stop the spread of her inside, using mainly a thorough analysis, a type of self-rated values, for the clarification of ideas, because knowing the causes of depression, it is possible to dissipate it very easily and shift its focus all your mental energy.

She contributes to the individual to find and can better understand their origins, making it more stable and less susceptible to external changes, which are reflected in the customs and social trends on your back and that could unbalance it many times.

This decrease occurs influences the extent that he will realize that each stage of life has its meaning or its importance when moving towards maturity.

She appears as the basis of all our psychological problems.

Ultimately, all our mental, neurotic and psychotic disorders have their origin in anxiety, and other physical ailments, such as insomnia, headache, heart problems and pressure. The anxiety is not restricted to any particular stage of life or any group of people, their characteristics penetrates all human situations, and acts directly at the heart of our emotions.

She is not related to any specific object or attitude and almost always expressed as an unintelligible evil, meaning a mental restlessness, which seems to have no objectivity. Any more specific approach to the problem of anxiety, requires prior knowledge of the different forms in which it operates in our mind, ie, there are two ways of expression of anxiety in the mind, direct and indirect.

Direct causes and indirect psychic repression manifests as a result of this repression, resulting in an increasing inner tension reflected in the mind, without the mind has any definite knowledge of what is happening.

Finally, anxiety is an inevitable accompaniment within the development process of life and it is up to us through the art of living, the improvement of techniques and necessary for better integration between her abilities and this continual rebirth that is life.

The wisdom in human relations is the mark of a mature personality that leads to happiness in life and also to spiritual development.

It is essential to our well-being and inner growth. Our life is formed by several plans, a relative balance between them to have a productive and happy life is necessary.

For example, for an individual to build a successful career, not only just the know-how or the equipment they have, but weighs a lot for this success the quality of people he knows, ie that its future success will certainly not will simply be a product of how much skill he had, but mostly how he managed to harmonize with those people who at one time or another in their professional lives, participated in contributing or slowing it your way.

When developing the skill in dealing with people within your convivial, the possibility of fluctuations decreases very emotional.

On the other hand when you have this skill, your problems are sure to multiply, leading you to alienation and social antagonism, the pressure will be much higher, hurting its minimum balance that is so necessary for their constructive development and spiritual fulfillment.

It happens because the fundamental purpose of human life is essentially linked to the concept of human relationships and the more she realizes this essence, becomes clearer your vision of cosmic prosperity, resulting in a much more meaningful and fruitful social life.

Depression along with the hurt and the like are afflictions of the mind and may disappear without reaching the level of despair, but this goes much deeper, affecting the very core of human existence.

She is an emotional disorder, a disease of the mind, more or less transient, despair is much more chronic is a sickness of the soul. All these states causes suffering, universally experienced, creating a natural impulse among all living creatures, in order to always avoid it.

When we think of the pain always comes a somewhat derogatory connotation, a negative fact. In contrast, when we think of the pleasure everything changes, because it is the goal of all normal efforts, being indispensable for the state of happiness ingredient and therefore humans suffer more intensely when it becomes aware of his own limitations.

However, his deepest suffering in a paradox, is also its moment of greatest joy. In the act of clearly recognizing its limitations, in a sense, he himself transcends all limitations and sees unlimited who dwells deep inside of her being surrounded by numerous limitations.

Thus pain and pleasure come together in this exalted moment of enlightenment, defining as the supreme goal of life, a dynamic that integrates itself happiness, pain and pleasure.

Moderation: when passion and reason, nature and the spirit must be driven by a dynamic harmony. Without the guidance of reason, a life is lost in passion auto dissipation, in the chaos of conflicting impulses, which are reflected in spirit.

Corporal discipline: when the body has to be prepared as a tool to search for a deeper spiritual life.

Concentration: it is an essential step in meditation and is to mobilize the resources of the mind in one direction, focusing mental energy on a defined target.

Self-observation: is the time of abandonment, the complete relaxation. We left the body and the mind in freedom and decided to do nothing. Discernment: consisting in concentration and self observation impartial, seeking relief from the stresses and strains of everyday life, involving relaxation and self emptying.

Lighting: without it, meditation reduces to a futile exercise because it represents the soul of meditation, is the perception of being.

Dedication: This is the final stage of meditation and consists of an active dedication to cosmic prosperity, representing the time that the perception of his being is integrated with the universe.

Some walk the trails, it is the sensibility that dominates, it is what governs your goals, very damaging to your emotional stability, preventing more objective judgments of facts, finally a slave sensitivity.

Fill their lives with dreams, daydreams, but dreaming life, not living it.

You need to move on, but if you use it, it is good to dream, but only as a motivator of action.

The dreams help us to trace goals, life goals, but in return also frustrates us, disappoint us and mess with our very emotional, which is the most vital aspect of human personality.

He covers the one hand, the instinctive impulses of nature and the other includes noble sentiments.

The individual can achieve a great intellectual superiority and yet remain emotionally a baby.

The emotional balance and maturity are essential ingredients for self-development, but for this purpose, we have to acquire an intimate knowledge of ourselves, we have to set limits on our impulses, desires and dreams, trying to realize them in such a rational way and organized as possible. Since childhood the circumstance of death is a fact that attracts our attention, whether we like it or not.

.

We cannot live indifferent to it, because the whole structure of our life is based on this phenomenon. However, most people seek to move away from this issue, so terribly disturbing, creating an immense emotional and unresolved that torments the individual throughout his life, paralyzing his initiative and smothering his spirit, causing intense emotional fluctuations.

The death in the mind operates like a black question mark and how the individual solves this question in your mind determines your whole way of living and therefore is an issue that has to be solved first of all, each must research, exchange ideas and find your truth to this phenomenon as natural and intriguing life.

It is the harmony. When the whole existence becomes unified, in which all the apparent contradictions are reconciled. There can be no happiness without proper self-development, as there are many conflicting tendencies in our nature.

A painful mistake is to take this or that desire too far, never give utmost importance to this or that aspect of life at the expense of all others. Should be first and foremost a self intelligent organization within our lives, which is the fundamental principle for achieving a balanced life.

We always have a multitude of desires, apparently conflicting and intertwined in our minds, there are different primitive, rational, selfish, altruistic impulses and give everyone always seeking to be administered as a goal the spirit of intelligent cooperation between nature and spirit, for without spirit nature is blind and the crippled nature of the spirit is finally in life, happiness can be achieved only when it follows the law of proper distribution, which is the operating principle of the concept of harmony. In this great adventure that is life, we expect a miracle every day, but we forget that this miracle is within ourselves, life itself.

We live in a bath of sensations, of which a small part attracts our attention and that we seek in religion, art and science, the great meaning of life, but experience teaches us that not all paths are for all walkers .

This is because some forget to help your inner dawn to sunrise and end up living a dull existence, that does not mean success or money, but simply a balanced and well-lived life.

Our reality is almost always less dramatic than the view we take of it, we must always be vigilant an optimist, renewing our energies at any moment, purifying our thoughts with a healthy imagination, always seeking to maintain vigorous and quiet mind, after all into the skin, all problems are psychological.

To the optimist, what matters is that now, at this very moment, are born, growing opportunities rich and pure, that the noblest essence of life doth flow in millions of people in all parts of the world, for those of us has the privilege of losing the flow, captures the vibrant life that only manifest through positivism therefore always be positive, upbeat, optimistic, cheerful, emotional fluctuations that are increasingly distant from your heart and your life .

Start your day always visualizing "I will have a day full of happiness," and make reality work in your favor.

The ultimate goal of life is harmony.

When the whole existence becomes unified, in which all the apparent contradictions are reconciled.

There can be no happiness without proper self-development, as there are many conflicting tendencies in our nature.

A painful mistake is to take this or that desire too far, never give utmost importance to this or that aspect of life at the expense of all others.

We always should seek to be above all an intelligent self-organization within our lives, which is the key to actually get a really balanced, happy and friendly life principle.

We always have a multitude of desires, apparently conflicting and intertwined in our minds, there are different primitive impulses, rational, selfish, altruistic, among others and all should be well managed as the primary goal always looking for the intelligent spirit of cooperation between nature and spirit, for without the spirit nature is blind and the crippled nature spirit is finally in life, happiness can only be achieved when you follow the law of the appropriate distribution, which is the operating principle of the concept of harmony.

When we look between the lines of this great adventure that is life, hope every day some kind of miracle, but we forget that this miracle is within ourselves, life itself. We live in a bath of sensations, of which a small part attracts our attention and that we seek in religion, art and science, the great meaning of life, but experience teaches us that not all paths are for all walkers .

This is because some forget to help your inner dawn to sunrise and end up living a dull existence, that does not mean success or money, but simply a balanced and well-lived life.

Our reality is almost always less dramatic than the view we take of it, we must always be vigilant an optimist, renewing our energies at any moment, purifying our thoughts with a healthy imagination, always seeking to maintain vigorous and quiet mind, after all the skin into all psychological problems are, what matters is that now at this very moment, are born, growing opportunities rich and pure, that the noblest essence of life doth flow in millions of people in all parts of the world because who among us has the privilege of losing the flow, captures the vibrant life that only manifest through positivism therefore always be positive, upbeat, optimistic, cheerful, emotional fluctuations that are increasingly distant from their heart and your life.

Start your day always visualizing "I will have a day full of happiness" and make reality work in your favor.

.

It is so charming who wins the grace of God and men.

There is nothing so lovely as a virtue, not as obnoxious as the addiction.

Virtue is not authentic; everything else is imitation.

Ability and greatness is measured by virtue, not by luck.

Virtue alone is sufficient to itself.

Love makes us remember the living and the dead.

The fear of the Lord is the beginning of knowledge, but fools despise wisdom and discipline.

Fuck whoever do not like me, I am what I am today and I'm proud.

If the world comes from?

You can see that I'm waiting with clenched fists!

Agora de uma coisa eu tenho certeza, assim como os perfumes alegram a vida, a amizade sincera dá animo para viver. Um brinde a renovação!

LIFE LESSONS FROM THE MONK

Not everything must be speculation: it takes action. The wisest are the easiest to fool: though they know extraordinary things, ignorant, know nothing of the ordinary necessities of life. The contemplation of sublime things leaves no room for the ordinary, and, as they ignore the basic things of life - where all the others are so insightful - or are admired, or are considered by the ignorant vulgar superficial. Therefore, the sages have a bit of traders, not enough to be duped and ridiculed. All that your hand finds to do, do it with all your heart. Learn be practical: it cannot be the highest concern of life, but it is most needed. What good is knowledge if it is not practical? Who is wise seeks to learn, but fools are satisfied with your own ignorance. When wisdom enters into your heart, and knowledge is pleasant to your soul, Discretion shall preserve thee, and keep thee intelligence. Nowadays, true knowledge is in knowing how to live. Do not confuse the taste of others. Causing grief rather than pleasure. Some try to please and end up harassing, because they do not understand the character of others. The same thing that flatters offends some others. What was considered a favor turns into grievance. Sometimes, it would have cost less pleasing than bored. Lose the gratitude when it is unknown how to please others. If you do not understand someone's character, you can not satisfy him. That's why some thought be praising when in fact insulted: a well-deserved punishment. Others plan to please with eloquence, when in reality bore the soul of others with his loquacity. Not trust his own reputation without pawning other people's honor. The damage for talking too much and the advantages of silence should be reciprocal. When honor is involved, the deal should be together, and must ensure the reputation of another. It is best not to rely on others, but if you do, it is with art, so he yields space for prudence and caution. Divide the risk to both follow the same interest and confidant does not become a witness against you. If you let the ax missed the cut and not the edge, will have to work much harder. It is smarter to plan before acting. Know how to ask. There is nothing more difficult for some and easier for others. There are those who can not deny; it does not take a lock pick to deal with them. Others have not always to first response, in which case it required skill. With all of them, act timely. Surprise them when they are happy, after delighting the mind and the body. However, it may occur to be alert enough to realize his intention. The days of rejoicing are those likely to grant favors; for the joy flows from the inside to the outside. Do not come closer to see someone have something denied because there is no longer afraid to say no. Also do not get anything from the sad. Making another part grateful beforehand is an exchange that the villains do not match. Turn favors prizes. It is of great political dexterity. Before granting favors to reward merit proves to be a good man. Anticipated favors are doubly advantageous: the speed of the giver who receives more forces, and the same gift, which would be debt becomes credit. It's a subtle way to reverse the obligations, for what should be a duty to reward the top became a burden to be met by contemplated. The strategy works only with good men. Among rogues, anticipating the reward acts as a brake, not as a spur. Remember that many are the plans in a man's heart, but what prevails is the Lord's purpose. The study is the essence of wisdom. Never share your secrets with his superiors. Think feathers share, but share stones. Many perished by being confident. They were like spoons made of crust of bread, and exposed to the same risk. Listen confidences of a prince is not a privilege, but a burden. Many break the mirror that reminds one of ugliness. Not bear to see those who see them. You will not be well seen if he saw something bad. Anyone owe us a lot of obligation, especially powerful. But if so, it is more for benefits that provide them with what they did favors for us. The confidences of friends are all dangerous. Who reveals his secrets to another becomes his slave, and such a sovereign does not support constraint for long. To regain the lost freedom, pass over everything, even reason. Do not forsake thee the kindness and faithfulness bind them around your neck write them upon the table of thine heart, and thou find favor and good understanding before God and men. Secrets, for, nor hear, nor reveal them. Know the piece that is missing. Many people would be complete if they lacked something they need to reach the height of perfection. Some would take care of it very little. Some lack of seriousness, which detract talent. Other lack of smoothness, which lacks the next immediately feel, especially when hold power. Some lack of activity, and other weighting. If you noticed, these defects could be easily supplied; because care can make the habit a second nature. Do not be too keen. It is better to be prudent. Like a gold ring in a pig's snout, so is a fair woman which is without discretion. If you know more than you ought, you lose the point: this is what happens with ordinary cunning. Seated truth is safest. Good to have understanding, but not pedantic. Do not forsake wisdom, and she will preserve you; Love her, and she will protect you. Much argument constitutes a kind of controversy. It is preferable to have a substantial discretion argue that necessary. Do not say without thinking, to say what you think. Do know is foolish. Even the wisest person sometimes makes use of this piece, and there are times when it is best to know is does not appear to have any. Should not be ignorant, just pretend to be. Wisdom does not matter for fools, and the wisdom to fools. So, talk to each his own language. Fool is not the one who pretends to be, but he who suffers it, because there is no true folly where comes the fireworks. In order to be admired by others, use a skin ass. Allow teasing, teasing but not the other. Endure a joke is an elegant act, but practice it can be provocative. What shows up in a grumpy party is an even bigger beast than it appears. Jokes are nice well-made, and how to accept them is a test of their ability. Showing up angry, you cause others to bored again. It is best to not connect and the safest is to take no notice. The most serious consequences of pranks ever arose. There is nothing that requires more attention and dexterity. Before you start, know as the nature of the other is able to tolerate. Complete the victories. Who refuse to hear the cry of the poor, he too will cry and not be heard. Some start everything and nothing ends. Fickle character, begin, but never persist. Never get praise because not proceed with anything. To them all before time ends. For some, it is born of impatience, which is typical of Spanish, as well as the Belgian is known for patience. The last things complete, the first ends of them; sweat to overcome the difficulty, content to win, but do not know complete victory.

Prove they can but do not want. It is a defect: levity shows, or disability. If the contract is worth, compensates finish. It compensates not finish, why start? The wise are not limited to stalking the prey; fells down. Columbian not be fully. The cunning of the serpent to alternate with the candor of the dove. There's a line that says. "Do not believe me do not you and important to mim.Quando no longer believe that I am important to you" Nothing is easier than to fool a good man; who never lies and the one who trusts will never deceive. Being deceived is not always a sign of foolishness; sometimes reveals kindness. The wise man hides his wisdom, the fool announces its ignorance. Two types of people prevent themselves from danger: the escarmentados, who learned at his own expense, and shrewd, who learned much at the expense of others. You need to be as shrewd as if in distrust is cunning in escaping the wiles. Not be good enough to give others the opportunity to be evil. Be mix of snake and dove; not a monster but a prodigy. Make the other debtors. Some transform himself into the favor of others: or give the impression they understand that grant a favor when in reality they are getting. Some are crafty that seem to grant honors to ask a favor; and honor others with the benefits they get. Arrange things so they seem to be having work to receive service, reversing, with such a ruse, the order of the bonds. Create doubt as to who favors those who, buy the very best with praise only. By showing that like something, give honor and flattery. Assert their rights on the courtesy of others, turning into debt so that should feel grateful. Change so the verb force from passive to active, and are better in politics than in grammar. This is a great subtlety, but subtlety is even greater surprise someone practicing it: undo the change, give them back their respects and regain the advantage. Argue sometimes unique way. It is proof of a superior talent. Not estimate who never opposed to it because it does so love yourself. Do not be fooled by flattery: not the reward, damn them. Consider an honor to be reproached, particularly by those who speak evil of good people. Be your grief if their actions are pleasing to all; is a sign that they are not good, because perfection is few. Do not give satisfaction to those who did not. And even when you ask, it's silly to give it beyond the request. Be excluded before it is asked to incriminate himself, and bleed yourself when you're healthy is to call itself malaise and malice. Apologizing beforehand awakens dormant suspicions. Cautious show never understand other people's suspicions: it would look offense. Try to disprove them with a correct behavior. Prepared for disappointment, ready to overcome, believing in the victory ... Knowing a little more, live a little less. Some people think the opposite. Better a good leisure than any business. Nothing belongs to us beyond time, the only abode of those who are homeless. Life is precious, and it is so unfortunate waste it on lofty tasks. Do not overload nor occupations, nor envy. Without wood a fire goes out;

without gossip a quarrel is over. You run over to smother the life and spirit. Some extend this rule to learn, but who does not know does not live. Do not be obsessed by the latter. The impertinence is always in extremes, and there are men who believe only in the last thing they heard. Your senses and desires are made of wax: the last print your brand, erasing all others. We can never have them as gains because they are easily lost; each of the tinge of his color. Confidants are bad: children who never grow up. Ranging in judgments and affections are always floating, with the will and being lame, losing there or here. Do not begin to live where it should end. There are four mysterious things that I can not understand: Eagle flying in the sky, the snake crawling on the rocks, the ship that finds its way into the sea and the love between a man and a woman. Some rest at the beginning, leaving fatigue towards the end. Make yourself the essentials first, then if there is time, the accessory. Some want the victory before the fight. Others start with learning what matters least and postpone until the end of life what could bring them fame and credit. Still others fade when no sooner began to make his fortune. Having method is essential to know and be able to live. The fear of the Lord is the beginning of knowledge. When arguing backwards? Those looking for wisdom loves life, and who acts intelligently finds happiness. When we speak with malice. With some, everything must be in reverse: yes is no and no is yes. If you criticize something, understands that hold him in high esteem. Why covet it for themselves, try to discredit him with the others. Not all praise is to speak well. Others avoid praising praising the good the bad. Although he does not consider that there will be no evil of having no good. Use human means as though divine did not exist, and divine means as if there were no humans. A great teacher gave such advice, which needs no comment. Not live entirely to themselves or to others fully. It is a common type of tyranny. If you want to have entirely to yourself, you will want to have it all to yourself. Who does not know is how to assign, or in the smallest things, or even lose a small portion of your convenience. Few solicitous trust your luck, which often leaves them. Should belong to others from time to time, so that others may belong to us. Who has a public office must be a public slave. Or carry the burden, or withdraw from office, as the old lady said Adriano. Unlike some people is totally other, since the folly always commits excesses, and this is a very unfortunate kind of excess. Do not have one day, not an hour for you, dedicate themselves completely to the other, the point that one of them was called "all". Even with the understanding that there are to know and for you all ignore. The wise understand that no one looking, but each seeks his own interest, and what you can do for him. Do not easily understand. Like apples of gold in settings of silver Is a word spoken in its time. Most do not esteem that which understands and worships you do not understand. To have value, things need to be difficult, if not have understood the more highly. To gain respect, show up wiser and more prudent than would be necessary for the proper interlocutor. But do it in moderation. The perceived value the wisdom, but with others as well is certain grandeur: keep them deciphering his message, and do not give them the opportunity to criticize him. Without much praise they can say whatever. Venerate all that is hidden or mysterious, because they hear praise and praise. Do not despise evil for being small. It never comes alone, but always in jail, like happiness. Seen a man diligent in his business? Will stand before kings; not remain between the lower position;. luck and bad luck usually go where there are already, and all flee and join the unlucky lucky. Even the doves, despite all the ingenuity, fly to the whitest tower. Unlucky to miss everything: lacks himself, his reason and any kind of comfort. Do not wake the chance when asleep. One stumble does not mean anything at first, but this follows the fall aimlessly fatal. For as any good is complete, no harm is totally over. To the misfortune sent by heaven, patience, and the terrain caution. Learn to do good. A little at a time, but often. Do not create more obligations than you can repay. That does not give that much, sell. Does not cover thanks therefore seeing themselves unable to thank the debtor breaks retribution. To lose friends, just make them too; to not have to pay for, move away, turning into enemies. The idol does not want to see the sculptor that he carved, and he that receiveth a favor rather not see the eyes of the benefactor. So learn this lesson about giving subtle: it costs very little and want to enjoy it more. Be forewarned against the coarse, stubborn, conceited and all kinds of fools. There are a lot of them, and prudence is in avoiding them. Arm yourself for daily purposes before the mirror of his prudence and thus win the bids of folly. Stay on guard and not expose their reputation in ordinary occurrences. Those who are in possession of good sense are not attacked by impertinence. Hitting the course on humane treatment is difficult, because it is full of protruding choices that our reputation is at risk. The safest is to change the course, appealing to the cunning of Odysseus. A soft answer calms wrath, but a harsh word increases anger. Here we have much value the feigned carelessness. And, above all, cost is free, the shortest way to stay away from complications. Never reach the breakup. Or your reputation will be ruined. Whoever loves discipline loves knowledge; but he that hateth reproof is brutish. All make good enemies, but few are good friends. Throughout time friend loves, and anguish is his brother. Few are capable of good, and almost all evil. On the day broke with the beetle, nor the eagle felt safe nestled in the bosom of Jupiter. At the break, by the hand of declared enemies, will stir the ire of hidden, awaiting the opportunity. Friends who offend become our worst enemies attack us with their own defects associated to ours. Others to see us break up with someone, speak as they feel and feel as they desire. Criticize all, whether at the beginning of friendship, for lack of prudence, or the end, for having waited so long. If unavoidable disruption, that is excusable: prior to the coldness of favors with a violent explosion. It is here that comes in handy on the stylish maximum withdrawals. Find someone to help bear the misfortunes. Never be alone, much less at risk, and not have to endure all the hate. Some want to take the upper hand, and all that is able to carry all the criticism. So, have a partner who can forgive him or help him endure adversity. Lord uncovers my eyes that I may behold wondrous things out of thy law. Eternal are the memories that touches the heart illuminating the longing of those who went away leaving marks of love, heal chest, but faith will gradually heal the pain of what is hopeless. Holistically it leads me to believe that the day I leave, I will surely rediscover all those who loved him. All things are full of labor and when the man can not speak, your eye is not satisfied with seeing, nor the ear its fill of hearing. Many waters can not quench love, neither can floods drown it; a man would give all the substance of his house for love, it would utterly be contemned. Neither luck nor vulgarity dare to attack the two. Doctors, taking wrong in therapy, not err in consult someone who can help them carry the coffin. Does love is an illusion, a beautiful way of suffering for people who mostly are rotten and replaceable. I do not have the answer, but I know that would be a great misfortune if it were true, because sharing the burden and sorrow, bearing this chance alone, would be doubly unbearable. Beautiful words, there was a time when comoviam me, not anymore. We live in world of few compliments and many envious. This envy is sure to not be able to do the same. Therefore, it becomes of paramount importance, prevent injuries and trying to turn them into favors. It is more shrewd than avoid offending them To avenge this is requires great skill to turn a possible rival a confidant, meaning that those who have attacked his reputation, now have become their advocates. Leaves little time for the grievance who fills it with thanks. Transforming sorrow in pleasures is knowing how to live. Turn the malevolence in his own confidant. Not be totally other, and not have someone totally yours. Neither blood nor friendship, nor even the strongest sense of obligation is sufficient; because giving someone the affection is very different from giving you the will. The human being unlearned feeling, standing up in the thrill. The union admits innermost exception; not so offended the laws of courtesy. All live sentimental frustrations until we become minimally able to exercise affectivity and construction practices that determine success in life together. If all things in reduce to zero, there is zero, we have to leave. A friend keeps to himself a secret and neither son reveals everything to his father. Some things are silent and speak with each other and vice versa, so that conceal and reveal all all, but for different confidants. Not persist in folly. Some insist on error, because they began to err, it seems to follow them perseverance as well. Basically, recognize their mistake, but with the others defend him; when started with the folly were seen as reckless as they continue, are confirmed as fools. Neither thoughtless promise nor wrong decision should compel us astray. Some people insist on initial stupidity and continue with their ineptitude. Fools want to be faithful. Learn to forget is another gift that arte.Aquilo what else should we forget is what we remember more easily. Memory is not only treacherous and not bailing failure when necessary, it is also foolish, resorting when they ought not. It causes pain when we prolix, and sloppy when you can give us pleasure. Sometimes, the best remedy for the evil would forget it, but we forget the remedy. Should therefore be instructing the memory to have better habits, because it alone can give us heaven or hell. Satisfied excetuamos in your foolish innocence, are always happy. Many nice things are better when they belong to someone else. You leverages the best that way. On the first day the pleasure belongs to the possessor; then others. When things belong to others, we we enjoy the double: without the risk of damage, and the pleasure of novelty. Anything tastes better when we are deprived of it; seems oblivious to the water nectar. Owning things, and profit decrease, increases the hassle of having to either lend them as not lend them. When we have things actually keep to the others, and are more enemies that require permission to use them than grateful. Not days of carelessness. Luck likes to play pranks, and not lose the opportunity to catch him off guard. The intelligence, prudence, value, up to the beauty are always put to the test, since the day we loose the attention will be the day of disrepute. The care is always more lacking when it is most needed, and thinking is not tipping in the undergrowth. The alien uses such attention ploy, catching qualities in our neglect to subject them to a rigorous examination. Knowing the days of display, the shrewdness let them pass. But the day when least expected is chosen to test its value. Knowing engage dependents. A push at the right time, transformed many personalities as well as the risk of drowning swimmers do. Thus many have discovered how much they value and how much they knew, otherwise all this would have continued sepulto in her shyness. Are those that are the trouble opportunity to gain fame, and a noble person, when to do justice to the honor, acts more than a thousand. This lesson, like many others, was full command of Isabel the Catholic Queen. The Great Captain owes its renown to such political favor, and many others, to eternal fame. This subtlety has made great men. Not bad due to excessive kindness. It's what happens to those who never gets angry. Who feels nothing has no personality. Such an attitude is not only due to insensitivity, but also disability. Feel intensely, when circumstances require, is an act of personal affirmation. Even the birds mock scarecrows. Switch the bitter with the sweet taste reveals: the sweetness alone is for children and fools. It is a great evil is lost for being so insensitive even being good. Gentle words, spoken gently. The arrows pierce the body: the bad words, the soul. A good treat gives good breath. Sell air is a subtle skill. Most things payable with words, and they alone are sufficient to accomplish the impossible. Trade up in the air with the air, and the breath encourages much higher. You always have a mouthful of sugar pastry for the words apeteçam up to his enemies. The only way to be kind is to be meek. The wise do in the beginning what fools leave later. Both do the same; the difference is at the moment. The first act in a timely manner, the latter not. If already started chocking understanding backwards, you do everything else the same way: kill underfoot that which should have kept the head, swapping right at left, being awkward to carry around. There is only one way to account things: as soon as possible. Otherwise it will thank you could have done with pleasure. The discreet logo see what has to be done sooner or later, and does so with pleasure, with advantage to his reputation. Take advantage of novelty. While it is new, will be estimated. The novelty appeals to everyone because of its variety and renews the taste. A rising mediocrity is estimated more than usual sumidade. The excellences suffer wear and end up aging. Note however that the novelty is short lived glory. In four days, we lost him the respect of the firstfruits. Take advantage of estimates and grab what you can during this fleeting pleasure. For the past enthusiasm for novelty, cool the passions, and pleasure turns into boredom. And believe:

all things have their time, and passed. Do not be the one to condemn what appeals to many. Something good must have since it appeals to so many. And, unless one understands, appreciates. The singularity is always obnoxious when erroneous, ridiculous. Your concept is discredited before the object; and remain alone with your bad taste. If you do not know how to see what is good in things, disguise their ineptitude, and not condemn overlooked; because the bad taste usually comes from ignorance. What everyone says or is or wants to be. In any profession, if you know little, stick to the safest. Although it is not seen as intelligent, will consider it justified. He who knows may be exposed to risks and indulge in fantasy, but take risks without knowing anything is wanting to fall off the cliff. Keep right; what is experienced can not fail. Follow the main road who does not know the way; In any case, knowing how much of the bypass, it is more sensible to the safety of eccentricity. Conquering things for the price of free. Make others more required. The applicant's request will never get to where the rich are willing to grant, even if you must must. Courtesy does not simply require the more reciprocity, and gallantry is the greater obligation. For the good man is nothing more expensive than what is given freely; is winning twice two prices: the value itself and courtesy. Truth is that for those who are bad, gallantry is empty talk because they do not understand the language of manners. Understand the character of the people we treat. To grant them the intentions. When well-known cause is known the effect. The effect reveals the reason. The melancholy always bode misfortunes and the slanderer, defects. Always think the worst, ignore the ever-present evil and announce possible. Who is dominated by passion not speak things as they are in reality: it speaks to passion, not reason. Each speaks as his affections or his humor, and all are far from the truth. Learn to decipher a face and figure through the features, of the soul. Know that one who always laughs is a fool, and he who laughs is never a fake. Beware the questioner, whether by being indiscreet, or because it is criticizing. Expect some of which have physical defects, for they love to take revenge of nature by having them honored so little. Normally the silliness is proportional to the beauty. Be sympathetic, because the attraction is a politically courteous spell. The gun courtesy captivate the goodwill of others, and also their services. Not enough to merit if not in valermos pleased - this is what it maketh approval which is the most subtle tool to lead others. Falling in good graces is a matter of luck, but it can be promoted by artifice, which picks up best when natural gifts are present. Sympathy leads to benevolence and, finally, the universal grace. Condescending, but not indecent. Do not show seriously and always bored: it is a matter of good manners. It should give a little decorum on to win the general affection. Sometimes, one can adopt the behavior of the majority, but do it without losing the decency: he that is taken by a fool in public will not be taken by wise in particular. Lose yourself in a day of euphoria more than it earned with years of complete seriousness. Should not always be different because being eccentric is to coordinate others.

"Dans le silence et la solitude, on n'entend plus que l'essentiel."

INFORMATION AND PUBLICATIONS

Twitter: Autor_Wladimir